Essential Viewpoints

EXTREMIST
GROUPS

Essential Viewpoints

EXTREMIST GROUPS

BY HAL MARCOVITZ

Content Consultant
Eric Mogren, JD, PhD
Associate Professor of History
Northern Illinois University

ABDO
Publishing Company

CREDITS

Published by ABDO Publishing Company, 8000 West 78th Street, Edina, Minnesota 55439. Copyright © 2009 by Abdo Consulting Group, Inc. International copyrights reserved in all countries. No part of this book may be reproduced in any form without written permission from the publisher. The Essential Library™ is a trademark and logo of ABDO Publishing Company.

Printed in the United States.

Editor: Paula Lewis
Copy Editor: Nadia Higgins
Interior Design and Production: Ryan Haugen
Cover Design: Emily Love

Library of Congress Cataloging-in-Publication Data
Marcovitz, Hal.
  Extremist groups / by Hal Marcovitz.
      p. cm. — (Essential viewpoints)
  Includes bibliographical references and index.
  ISBN 978-1-60453-108-4
  1. Radicals—United States. 2. Radicalism—United States. 3. Hate groups—United States. I. Title.

  HN90.R3M345 2009
  305.5'680973—dc22

                                      2008006993

TABLE OF CONTENTS

*Toledo, Ohio, Mayor Jack Ford speaks at a press conference
following a white supremacist march on October 15, 2005.*

THE RIGHT TO BE HEARD

or more than a century, extremist groups
have surfaced in U.S. society. These
groups represent a broad range of people who
often harbor inflammatory views, particularly in
political matters. What defines such a group often
depends on the historical and social contexts of the

group's actions. What today's society might consider "extreme" may have been acceptable, or at least tolerated, at other points in history. Equally, what we applaud today may have been considered extreme in the past. Such groups have included racists, such as neo-Nazis and members of the Ku Klux Klan. Communists and anarchists have advocated the overthrow of the U.S. government. Other groups include radical antiabortion activists, some members of the animal rights movement, militiamen, and Islamic extremists. Knowing when a group's ideas are considered extreme is not as easily defined.

The U.S. Constitution's provisions for free speech and assembly apply to everyone, regardless of the messages. Sometimes, however, extremist groups spark intensely passionate emotions in others. These emotions make citizens question the extent of the Constitution's guarantees. At times, the debate has made it difficult for authorities to ensure that basic constitutional rights are respected.

A Confrontation

In October 2005, an extremist group of neo-Nazis known as the National Socialist Movement (NSM) scheduled a march. The NSM selected

What Is a Swastika?

The swastika symbol is a hooked cross. It was first used in contexts and cultures different from the Nazis. Depending on the culture, it symbolizes abundance, prosperity, and Buddha's heart.

The swastika is *haken-kreuz* in German. During World War I, the symbol was adopted by members of a German brigade who wore it on their helmets. In 1920, the swastika was selected as the symbol of the National Socialist Party by Adolf Hitler, the party's founder. Hitler sought to dominate the world by exterminating races he regarded as inferior. Since the end of World War II, it has been illegal to display the swastika in Germany. However, under U.S. law, displaying the symbol is protected by the First Amendment.

a multiracial neighborhood in Toledo, Ohio, to stage its demonstration. The neo-Nazi leaders claimed they organized the event to show support for the white residents of the neighborhood. Reportedly, the residents had been victims of violence by African-American gang members.

During the press conference that preceded the march, the neo-Nazis made several racial slurs. In retaliation, African-American youths and others threw rocks and debris at the neo-Nazis. Although the extremists were quickly taken away by police, rioting erupted.

Roberta de Boer is a newspaper columnist who attended the press conference. She stated that the NSM members clearly intended to incite the crowd, which included many African Americans.

They were ending their press conference when rocks, bottles, bricks

A neo-Nazi group staged a second protest at
Toledo City Hall in December 2005.

*began flying through the air . . . and the police decided
suddenly just to shut down the plan for the day. They whisked
the neo-Nazis away under police escort, but the crowds
continued to grow as the day went on. And the anger, really,
that was directed at the neo-Nazis then sort of transferred
over to the police and to anybody else who was around that
area, and things got quite out of control.*[1]

By the end of the day, police had arrested more than 100 people.

For the citizens of Toledo, the incident turned into a long and ugly confrontation that threatened to upset the city's racial harmony. Unfortunately, Toledo's involvement with extremism did not end on that October night. The NSM members insisted that their rights to free speech had been trampled by police who did not let them stage their march.

In December, the NSM returned to hold a rally in downtown Toledo. This time, police maintained order by keeping the crowd well back during the speeches. Still, minor scuffling in the crowd resulted in nearly 30 arrests.

Jack Ford, Toledo's mayor and an African American, was obligated by law to uphold the rights of racists to stage public rallies in his community. By providing a forum for the NSM, Ford was criticized by his African-American constituents. Toledo newspaper columnist de Boer commented,

> *When he waded into that crowd on Saturday afternoon and tried to calm things down, he did not get a warm reception. A lot of people said, "Man, you're black. You're one of us. Why did you let these neo-Nazis in here?"*[2]

The Heart of the Controversy

The First Amendment to the Constitution guarantees the rights of assembly and free speech. This means that members of extremist groups—no matter how offensive their messages—have the right to hold meetings or demonstrations and voice their opinions.

During the first incident in Toledo, the police were concerned with the safety of the marchers and the residents of the multiracial neighborhood. This led police to deny the NSM members their rights to free

The First Amendment

The First Amendment is one of ten amendments to the Constitution known as the Bill of Rights. The first ten amendments were drafted by James Madison in response to demands by political leaders that the Constitution include guarantees for personal freedoms.

The First Amendment states:

Congress shall make no law respecting an establishment of religion, or prohibiting the free exercise thereof; or abridging the freedom of speech, or of the press, or the right of the people peaceably to assemble, and to petition the Government for a redress of grievances.[3]

The First Amendment has provided extremist groups with the right to make racial slurs from a podium. The law has also permitted others to publicly make their controversial opinions known. For example, the courts have ruled that people who publicly burn the U.S. flag are protected by the First Amendment. Offensive comments by radio personalities are also protected. During the 1960s, filmmakers won the right to depict profanity, nudity, and violent acts in movies after a series of court challenges upheld their First Amendment rights to free expression.

Security in Toledo

To prevent rioting at the second NSM event in Toledo, the city won a court order limiting the neo-Nazi rally to a small section of downtown. The rally included 63 neo-Nazi members. Their speeches were witnessed by a crowd of 170, mostly counterdemonstrators. Security was maintained by 700 police officers from Toledo as well as nearby communities.

speech and assembly. However, audience members at the press conference who shouted down and threatened the activists also denied NSM its rights. As U.S. citizens, members of the crowd had the responsibility to respect the constitutional rights of the neo-Nazis, regardless of their personal feelings.

In the second incident in Toledo, the police also may have denied the rights of many people in the crowd to respond to the racist messages. Whenever people approached the stage, they were quickly taken into custody. "What you have in Toledo is martial law for a day," said Terry Lodge, a Toledo lawyer and civil rights activist. "The whole business of shoving people back preemptively is wrong."[4]

ON THE FRINGES

What occurred in Toledo is similar to what has happened over the years in dozens of other U.S. cities. Extremist groups such as the neo-Nazis, the Ku Klux Klan, and others know their speech is protected by the Constitution. They also know that the police will provide them with physical protection. Extremists have staged rallies and marches not only to stir up passions in the community but to enlist new members. They are well aware of the publicity that these events receive. Their messages will be reported in the press, posted on the Internet, printed in newspapers, and broadcast on radio and television.

Despite this media coverage, extremists have remained on the fringes of society. Often, their messages fall on deaf ears. Their occasional attempts to elect candidates to public office have generally failed. Few extremist groups have the resources to stay together for more than a few years. In many cases, funds dry up, organizations splinter because of internal disputes, or leaders are jailed. Although individual extremist groups may disband, many of the ideas that drive them remain unchanged. And, new issues or policies initiate new voices that support or challenge these concepts.

As Toledo's example shows, determining what type of behavior is acceptable has often tested people's tolerance. At times, extremist groups have

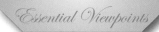

turned to violence. In those cases, the appropriate enforcement agencies have investigated the crimes and prosecuted those responsible. In other cases, the line between right and wrong has not been as clear. This led to varied interpretations of what is permissible under the law by the courts, the civil rights activists, and others with a deep interest in the issues presented by the extremists.

This building was set on fire during the October 15, 2005, riot that occurred in Toledo in connection with a neo-Nazi march.

*In 1925, Ku Klux Klan members march down
Pennsylvania Avenue in Washington DC.*

EXTREMISM IN
U.S. SOCIETY

Extremist groups have been a part of
U.S. society since the country's earliest
days. In 1798, John Fries of Pennsylvania organized
a group of several hundred fellow farmers who

opposed a new tax passed by Congress. For a year, Fries and his followers harassed tax collectors, often using violence. Finally, the governor dispatched the militia to arrest Fries and his men. They were tried and sentenced to be hanged. However, President John Adams pardoned them in 1800.

An extremist group is often identified by its actions. While controversial opinions and beliefs are generally protected by law, violent actions based on those beliefs are not. In 1866, six former Confederate soldiers from Tennessee founded the Ku Klux Klan to oppose rights granted to freed slaves. The Klan soon turned to violence, killing hundreds of African Americans over the next five years. In response, President Ulysses S. Grant dispatched federal troops into the South to arrest Klan leaders. Within a short time, the troops had destroyed the Klan and Klan leadership disbanded the group.

Rebirth of the Klan

In 1915, a major Hollywood film, *Birth of a Nation*, was released. The film portrayed the Klan as a noble organization that fought the oppression of innocent whites by evil African Americans.

The new Klan of the early 1900s was loosely organized, but it still made its opinion known. Klan members demonstrated in public, became influential in politics, and wielded power through violence. Lynching became the preferred intimidation method of the Klan, as well as other white racists, for terrorizing African Americans, Jews, Catholics, and others. These organized acts of violence set the Klan apart as an extremist group, even if lingering racism in U.S. society led many to agree with the group's beliefs.

Birth of a Nation

The 1915 film *Birth of a Nation* is believed to be responsible for rekindling the Ku Klux Klan movement in the United States. The movie, produced during the silent era of film, was directed by film pioneer D. W. Griffith. It was based on the book *The Clansman* by Thomas Dixon, a racist author from North Carolina.

The film and book tell the story of the South's struggles during the Civil War and Reconstruction. Klan members are portrayed as heroic freedom fighters protecting white southern women from murderous African Americans. The three-hour film was praised for its technical achievements. When President Woodrow Wilson was given a private screening in the White House, he declared, "It is like writing history with lightning, and my only regret is that it is all so terribly true."[1]

Others did not share the president's opinion. Leaders of the National Association for the Advancement of Colored People (NAACP) protested loudly. They tried several legal maneuvers to keep the film from opening. Their efforts fell short as judges and industry watchdog groups upheld the rights of the producers to release the film.

By the 1930s, antilynching laws helped imprison many Klan members and others who had taken such violent actions. Also leading to the downfall of the Klan was the 1925 murder conviction and imprisonment of Indiana Klan leader David Curtiss Stephenson. He was convicted of committing the brutal abduction and rape of a white schoolteacher that led to her death. The murder and trial resulted in considerable negative national attention. Stephenson's conduct also caused revulsion among Klan members. Many who believed their primary mission was to protect white women quit the organization.

In the 1940s, white supremacists were further weakened by their association with Adolf Hitler. Many Klan leaders and others publicly embraced Hitler's racist opinions. This alienated them from society at a time when young men joined the U.S. military to fight such ideas in Europe.

OTHER EXTREMISTS

While the Klan rose and fell, other dissident groups came forward. During the final years of the nineteenth century, socialist agitators found support among the poor European immigrants of the northern cities. Their movement also turned violent at times.

Americans also heard other political voices. In 1901, anarchist Leon Czolgosz emerged from a crowd in Buffalo, New York, and assassinated President William McKinley. Later, in an interview with reporters, Czolgosz declared McKinley an enemy of working people. Two months after McKinley's assassination, Czolgosz was executed. Czolgosz acted alone, but many groups shared his ideas for a need to support the working class. The most influential group was the Industrial Workers of the World. Members included mine workers, dockworkers, lumbermen, and other laborers.

During World War I, the U.S. government took steps to clamp down on dissent. In 1917, Congress passed the Espionage Act and, a year later, an amendment known as the Sedition Act. These acts made it a crime to criticize or obstruct the war effort. Among the first to be arrested and convicted under the Espionage Act was Eugene Debs, head of the Socialist Party. He urged his followers to resist the draft. Because the political beliefs of socialism were not in favor at the time, many party members were victimized by mainstream society.

George Lincoln Rockwell, third from left, founder of the American Nazi Party, and his hate bus

In 1919, anarchists hurled bombs at various targets across the country. One target was the Washington DC home of Attorney General A. Mitchell Palmer. In retaliation, Palmer ordered a large number of searches and seizures of suspected communists, socialists, anarchists, and others. As a result of the "Palmer Raids," approximately 10,000

George Lincoln Rockwell

A former artist from Illinois, George Lincoln Rockwell was a veteran of World War II. He returned from the war with harsh anti-Semitic, anticommunist, and racist notions. In 1959, he organized the World Union of Free Enterprise and National Socialists. The name was soon changed to the American Nazi Party.

Rockwell gained national prominence by staging public rallies and giving press interviews. These included an interview that African-American journalist Alex Haley dramatized in the television series *Roots: The Next Generations*. In 1967, Rockwell was murdered by a former member of his party who was a suspected communist.

suspected political leftists were arrested under the Espionage Act and the Sedition Act, although the vast majority had committed no crime at all. However, 550 were deported to Europe and Russia. During these raids, federal agents worried little about civil rights. Agents barged into homes and offices without search warrants, beat confessions out of suspects, and jailed people on flimsy evidence. Palmer's actions seem extreme in today's context. However, at the time, they were supported by a broad number of Americans.

During the 1950s, Wisconsin Senator Joseph McCarthy, the U.S. House Un-American Activities Committee, and others, too, sought to purge U.S. society of people who disagreed with a capitalist or democratic state. McCarthy, Palmer, and others who took such drastic measures became extreme in their own efforts to persecute people who held less popular political beliefs.

Meanwhile, other groups also surfaced. During the 1950s, Ku Klux Klan chapters reappeared in response to gains African Americans were making in the civil rights movement.

In response, African-American activists Huey Newton and Bobby Seale established the Black Panther Party. They called upon African Americans to promote self-defense and socialism, using violent means if necessary. In 1959, George Lincoln Rockwell, an anti-Semite, founded the American Nazi Party. Rockwell and his swastika-wearing followers staged rallies in New York City and Washington DC. In 1968, Jewish radicals formed the Jewish Defense League. This group often resorted to violence as an answer to anti-Semitism. Their rallying cry was "Never Again!" This referred to the slaughter of 6 million Jews during World War II by Nazi Germany.

During the 1970s, a forerunner of the militia movement was the Posse Comitatus. Members of this group harbored suspicions about the government. They believed it was planning secret plots that targeted their civil liberties and that the government's system for income taxation was illegal. While a variety of groups act to protect civil liberties, the Posse Comitatus was involved in an assassination, which led the group to be associated with extremism.

In 1993, a bomb exploded in the parking garage of the World Trade Center in New York City, killing six people. Suddenly, U.S. citizens became aware of radical fundamentalist Muslims in the United States. This became even more apparent after the September 11, 2001, terrorist attacks on the World Trade Center in New York City and the Pentagon in Washington DC.

A Clear and Present Danger

Starting in the early twentieth century, dissident groups began to receive legal protection through the courts. A series of court decisions helped solidify their First Amendment rights as guaranteed under the Constitution. The courts defined the rights of dissidents to call meetings, speak their minds, and publish their views.

In 1919, the Supreme Court upheld the conviction of Charles Schenck. This decision was the beginning of a series of rulings that modified and shaped the nature of protected speech. A socialist,

Schenck had been arrested under the Espionage Act for distributing leaflets urging men to resist the draft. The court ruled that in times of war, the government did have a right to control speech. Although he upheld the ruling, Justice Oliver Wendell Holmes wrote that the government could stifle speech only when a "clear and present danger" existed.[2]

That same year, the Supreme Court issued a decision in another Espionage Act case. It upheld the conviction of Jacob Abrams, a socialist arrested for distributing antidraft pamphlets. This time, two justices—Holmes and Louis Brandeis—disagreed with the ruling. They found there was no clear and present danger in the Abrams case. In his dissenting opinion, Holmes wrote:

> *I think we should be eternally vigilant against attempts to check [suppress] the expression of opinions that we loathe and believe to be fraught with death, unless they so imminently threaten immediate interference with the lawful and pressing purposes of the law that an immediate check [restraint] is required to save the country.*[3]

Five decades later, the Supreme Court ruled that any form of speech should be tolerated as long as it did not urge a specific act of violence. In 1964, the ruling was put to the test when Ohio Ku Klux Klan leader Clarence Brandenburg made threats at a rally. He promised retaliation against the federal government for suppressing the rights of white citizens. Although Brandenburg intended to stir up the passions of his followers, he did not advocate a specific act of violence. Nevertheless, Brandenburg was arrested. He was convicted under an Ohio law that barred speech advocating illegal acts. In 1969, the Supreme Court unanimously voted to overturn Brandenburg's conviction. Their decision concluded that the Klan leader's speech presented no clear and present danger. ⌒

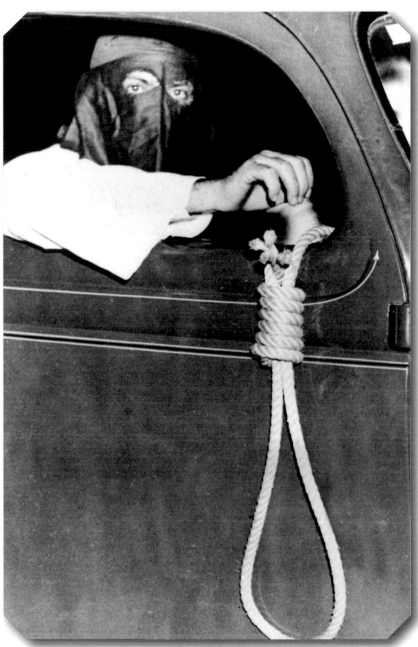

In 1939, a Ku Klux Klan member uses a scare tactic to warn African Americans to stay away from the polls.

Roger Baldwin founded the National Civil Liberties Union in 1917. The name was changed to the American Civil Liberties Union in 1920.

DEFENDING THE RIGHTS OF EXTREMISTS

The eighteenth-century French philosopher Voltaire was known for his tolerant political beliefs. The twentieth-century author Evelyn Beatrice, writing as S.G. Tallentyre, paraphrased Voltaire's tolerance as, "I disapprove of what you say, but I will defend to the death your right to say it."[1] These words also apply to people who believe passionately in the Constitution's guarantee of the right to free speech.

Lawyers from the American Civil Liberties Union (ACLU) often defend the civil rights of extremist groups. In part, this is because of the fact that other attorneys refuse to accept extremists as clients. Also, the ACLU generally does not charge fees for taking cases related to constitutional rights.

The ACLU is often considered to be the last line of defense against the government and institutions that seek to trample upon the First Amendment. The ACLU states that it

> *has been involved in virtually all of the landmark First Amendment cases to reach the U.S. Supreme Court, and remains absolutely committed to the preservation of each and every individual's freedom of expression.*[2]

The ACLU

The organization was founded by Roger Baldwin, a wealthy Boston attorney. Baldwin had been a farmer and a teacher before devoting his life to social activism. The ACLU's original mission was to provide legal representation to conscientious objectors. These were men who had refused to enter military service during World War I on the basis of their religious and personal beliefs. It also aided people arrested under the Espionage Act.

The ACLU's Communist Purge

In 1939, Europe was on the brink of war. Joseph Stalin was the leader of the Soviet Union (now Russia), a communist country. Stalin signed a nonaggression pact with Adolf Hitler of Nazi Germany. The two countries agreed not to attack each other. This cleared the way for the Nazi invasion of Poland and the start of World War II. ACLU founder Roger Baldwin, an ardent communist, was enraged by Stalin's actions. In response, Baldwin severed his ties with communism. He led a move in 1940 to purge communists from the ACLU's board.

GITLOW AND WHITNEY

In 1919, the ACLU accepted its first two free speech cases. In the first case, the ACLU represented Benjamin Gitlow, the business manager for the *Revolutionary Age*, a Socialist Party newspaper. An editorial in the paper suggested the overthrow of the democratic government and the establishment of a communist government. Gitlow was arrested under a New York State law that made it a crime to promote the overthrow of the U.S. government. The Supreme Court ruled that a state government could not deny a right guaranteed under the Constitution. However, the Supreme Court refused to overturn Gitlow's conviction. They found that the message in the *Revolutionary Age* had crossed over the "clear and present danger" line.

In the second case, the ACLU represented Charlotte Whitney. This California woman was convicted under a state law for helping to organize the Communist Labor Party. Her conviction was upheld as well. However, Justice Brandeis made it clear that Whitney had the right to publicly criticize the U.S. government. In his opinion, Brandeis wrote, "Those who won our independence by revolution were not cowards. They did not fear political change. They did not exalt order at the cost of liberty."[3]

In both cases, the Supreme Court upheld the convictions of the defendants. However, the ACLU still claimed victory. In issuing their opinions, the justices had drawn definitions for free speech. These definitions would later clear the way for the 1969 decision in favor of Ku Klux Klan leader Clarence Brandenburg.

BACKLASH AGAINST THE ACLU

Despite its accomplishments, the ACLU has experienced disagreement within its organization.

In 1977 the ACLU accepted a case that deeply upset many of its members. It came to the defense of neo-Nazis in a free speech case centered in Skokie, Illinois, a northern suburb of Chicago. Nearly half of Skokie's 70,000 residents were Jewish. This included approximately 1,200 people who had survived the Nazi concentration camps. In this racially mixed neighborhood, neo-Nazi Frank Collin had established the National Socialist Party of America with only a few followers.

Collin's group requested a parade permit to stage a march through Skokie. The town council turned

The March on Skokie

Frank Collin founded his National Socialist Party of America in response to a change in his southwest Chicago neighborhood. The all-white neighborhood had become racially mixed. He held numerous antiblack demonstrations in nearby Marquette Park that drew audiences of angry counterdemonstrators. In an attempt to avoid violence in the park, the Chicago City Council adopted an ordinance that required groups to post $250,000 insurance bonds to stage parades or demonstrations in city parks. Unable to raise the money for the insurance, Collin's neo-Nazi group announced plans to march in suburban Skokie instead.

In 1978, a federal court found that Skokie's refusal to grant the neo-Nazis a parade permit violated their First Amendment right to free speech. However, the march in Skokie never occurred. Armed with a court order, Collin staged a parade in downtown Chicago instead. During the event, hundreds of Chicago police officers escorted a weak turnout of neo-Nazis in a 15-minute parade. Thousands of counterdemonstrators lined the streets, shouting insults at the extremists.

*Frank Collin, seated, leader of the National Socialist Party
of America, at a press conference in June 1978*

down the request. With representation by the ACLU,
the neo-Nazis won a court order upholding the
group's right to free assembly and speech. This
became a precedent-setting case. In subsequent
years, other communities fought efforts by extremist
groups to stage rallies or marches in their cities. In
all cases, the courts upheld the constitutional rights
of the extremists.

Although the ACLU could claim a victory in a
First Amendment case, the organization's success
proved costly. Shortly after the verdict cleared the
way for the march, approximately 75,000 ACLU

The Burning Cross

Since its earliest years, the Ku Klux Klan has used a burning cross as a symbol. But what does the burning cross represent? Is it a symbol of free speech or a method of intimidation?

In 2002, the ACLU defended Klan member Barry E. Black, who was arrested under a Virginia state law banning cross burning. The ACLU attorney, David Baugh—an African American—argued that the burning cross was protected under the First Amendment. The Supreme Court disagreed.

members, mostly Jews, left the organization. This reduced the membership by 25 percent. With this loss in dues, the ACLU plunged into debt. At the time of the Skokie case, ACLU national director Aryeh Neir, a Jew, said he was constantly barraged with complaints from Jewish members asking, "How can you, a Jew, defend freedom for Nazis?"[4]

It took years for the ACLU to rebuild its membership. Despite the backlash by many of its Jewish members, the organization has continued to accept free speech cases. The ACLU represents neo-Nazis, Ku Klux Klan members, and other extremists who pledge their hatred for Jews, African Americans, and other minorities.

Leaders of the ACLU insist that the constitutional rights of these groups must be defended, even if their message may be offensive. Although controversial in its actions to defend unpopular groups, the ACLU continues to fight for equal constitutional and civil rights among all citizens.

The U.S. Supreme Court ruled that the burning of a cross
is not protected by the First Amendment.

7-2-99

Although I have not been a
member of the World Church
of the Creator since April 1999,
due ... ast public support
... religious organization
... Hale, I find it
... merly break
... Church or the
because I am unable t
to follow a legal
f values.

Benjamin ... Smith

Matthew Hale, founder of the World Church of the Creator, holds a letter written by Benjamin Nathaniel Smith requesting that the Illinois Supreme Court allow Hale to practice law.

CROSSING THE RHETORICAL LINE

Civil libertarians argue that everyone has the right to free speech as guaranteed by the First Amendment. However, the case of Benjamin Nathaniel Smith raises troubling questions about where the "clear and present danger" line can be drawn.

SINISTER INTENTIONS

The goal of the World Church of the Creator (WCOTC) and its members was to make the nation and the world entirely white. The WCOTC was known for crossing the line between words and violence. In 1995, WCOTC member John McLaughlin was arrested for stockpiling guns and other weapons. He told police he was preparing for the "ultimate race war."[1] Over the next three years, ten more members faced charges, most of which involved the use of violence against minorities.

In 1996, Matthew Hale became the head of the WCOTC. Hale and his members advocated a racial holy war, or a war against certain races and religions. Hale publicly maintained that the war could be fought nonviolently and within the confines of the law.

City Council Candidate

Matthew Hale never tried to hide his racist ideas. Over the years, he joined extremist groups and formed many of his own. He proclaimed himself National Leader of the National Socialist White Americans Party. In 1995, at the age of 23, he ran for a seat on the East Peoria City Council of Illinois. He did not win the election. Despite campaigning on a racist platform, he did receive 14 percent of the vote—a total that stunned many people in the close-knit community.

By the summer of 1999, it became clear that Hale's public statements contradicted the group's real intentions. The WCOTC had established itself as a violent organization. On the WCOTC's Web site, Hale listed the group's 16 commandments. These included a commitment to "destroy and banish all Jewish thought and influence" and the necessity for a "total solution to the ills of this planet."[2] These words brought to mind Adolf Hitler's "total solution"—the elimination of European Jews. "Hitler's program," Hale wrote, "is similar to what we are proposing."[3]

A History of Violence

The Church of the Creator (COTC) had been organized in 1973 by Florida racist Ben Klassen. In 1992, COTC leader George Loeb was convicted in the murder of Harold Mansfield Jr., an African-American Gulf War veteran. Loeb was sentenced to life in prison. In 1994, Mansfield's family filed suit against the COTC, claiming the group was responsible for his death. The court agreed and awarded Mansfield's family a judgment of $1 million. The judgment, and the leadership vacuum caused by Klassen's suicide in 1993, destroyed the COTC.

In 1996, with the COTC bankrupt and its leaders either dead or in prison, Matthew Hale stepped forward. He changed the group's name to the World Church of the Creator (WCOTC). He began to recruit members and soon drew Benjamin Nathaniel Smith into its ranks. In 2005, Hale was imprisoned on charges of attempted murder of a federal judge.

AN EAGER DISCIPLE

Hale and Benjamin Nathaniel Smith met in

1997 at the University of Illinois, where Smith was
a student. Hale visited the campus to recruit new
members for the WCOTC. He found Smith an eager
disciple of the group's mission.

Smith distributed racist literature. The university
tolerated Smith's actions, acknowledging his First
Amendment rights, but they watched him closely. By
early 1998, school officials found the justification
to kick him out: Smith had allegedly beaten up his
girlfriend as well as other students. He also had a
hidden collection of guns.

Smith soon enrolled at the University of Indiana.
He continued to distribute racist literature and
spread the WCOTC's message. It became clear that
Hale's public messages of a nonviolent agenda were
untrue. The group had far more sinister intentions.
In an interview, Smith said:

> *We believe we can come to power through nonviolence, but
> Hale says if they [officials] try to restrict our legal means then
> we have no recourse but to resort to terrorism and violence.*[4]

By the summer of 1999, Hale's reputation had
reached a panel of the Illinois State Bar Association.
As a law school graduate, Hale applied for admission
to practice law in Illinois. The bar association

"Creator of the Year"

In early 1999, the WCOTC named Benjamin Nathaniel Smith "Creator of the Year." This high honor was awarded to the WCOTC member who showed the most devotion to the group's racist agenda.

Six months later, Smith murdered two people and wounded nine others before killing himself.

committee heard testimony about Hale's fitness to do so. Smith testified on Hale's behalf.

During his testimony, Smith said that Hale had helped him to rein in his violent tendencies. The committee was not convinced. They also concluded that Hale lacked the moral character to serve as an attorney. In making its ruling, the bar committee stated:

While Matthew Hale has not yet threatened to exterminate anyone, history tells us that extermination is sometimes not far behind when governmental power is held by persons with his racial views.[5]

Only hours after the state bar turned down Hale's application to practice law, Smith began to interpret Hale's statements much more literally. Smith went on a murderous three-day rampage across Illinois and Indiana. He murdered two people and wounded nine others. Then he turned his gun on himself as police closed in. His victims were African Americans, Orthodox Jews, and a Korean American. Police suggested that Smith committed the murders

in retaliation for Hale's rejection from the Illinois
Bar. Hale claimed that he had no part in Smith's
actions.

Smith's shooting spree prompted debate over
whether Hale's incendiary language had gone too
far. The fact that Hale refused to express remorse for
Smith's victims spurred the debate. Harlan Loeb, an
attorney for the Anti-Defamation League, a Jewish
rights group, stated:

> On the one hand, free speech is a very, very important,
> probably essential piece of our democracy. . . . On the
> other hand, you can't always wrap yourself up in the First
> Amendment and immunize yourself from any further
> scrutiny.[6]

Hale had his defenders. Robert Herman, a
Missouri attorney specializing in First Amendment
law, believed the Illinois Bar Association had
rejected Hale's application on faulty grounds.
Herman petitioned them to repeal their decision.
If necessary, Herman planned to appeal the bar
association's decision. He insisted that Hale (who
was not charged in the Smith case) could not be held
responsible for Smith's murders, regardless of how
volatile his words may have been.

At the time of the murders, the WCOTC membership had grown to approximately 150 followers. Hale received national publicity and used his new "fame" to continue his recruitment efforts. But his insistence that the WCOTC's mission was nonviolent soon lost any shred of legitimacy. Following Smith's rampage, a legitimate Oregon-based religious group, known as the Church of the Creator, sued Hale. The group insisted that it held the legal rights to the name. U.S. Judge Joan Humphrey Lefkow ruled in favor of Hale. However, the decision was overturned on appeal. Hale was ordered to cease calling his racist organization the World Church of the Creator.

In retaliation, Hale planned Lefkow's murder. FBI agents had planted informers within the ranks of the WCOTC. They were able to intercede before Hale had the opportunity to carry out the plot. In 2005, Hale was convicted and sentenced to a prison term of 40 years. In sentencing Hale, U.S. Judge James Moody said, "I consider Mr. Hale to be extremely dangerous and the offense for which he was convicted to be extremely egregious."[7]

Matthew Hale, shown in a 1999 photo, was found guilty of planning the murder of Judge Lefkow.

*After a siege of 51 days, flames take over the Branch Davidian
compound near Waco, Texas.*

Is Force Justified?

As Matthew Hale's case shows, the line
between speech protected by the First
Amendment and speech that provokes a crime
can be hazy. Without Hale's ideas and efforts,
Benjamin Nathaniel Smith may not have found the
encouragement or justification to kill two people and

wound nine others. There is often debate over when and where government force is justified.

In a different case, law enforcement officials used force to shut down what they regarded as an extremist group engaged in illegal activities. In 1993, federal agents laid siege to a compound near Waco, Texas. The compound was occupied by a religious group known as the Branch Davidians. The 51-day siege resulted in numerous deaths as well as the destruction of the compound.

Coming Apocalypse

The Branch Davidians were a splinter group of the Seventh-day Adventist Church. They based their ideology largely on the idea that the apocalypse—the final confrontation between good and evil—was near. Amid this confrontation, Jesus Christ would return to Earth in what they called the Second Coming.

Branch Davidian founder Victor Houteff established the compound near Waco in 1934 as a place for his followers to await the Second Coming. In 1981, David Koresh, a semiliterate high school dropout, joined the group. By the 1990s, Koresh became the Branch Davidian's leader. Over the years, the Branch Davidians had become blindly devoted to

Koresh. They accepted his rule that he was the only member permitted to father children. Koresh is said to have had sexual relations with all 140 female members, including some as young as 12. In early 1993, local authorities heard rumors that Koresh had sexually assaulted minors in the compound, and social workers were sent to investigate.

At the compound, the social workers were barred from speaking with the children. Meanwhile, evidence surfaced that the Branch Davidians had stockpiled illegal weapons. When federal agents

The Branch Davidians

The Seventh-day Adventist (SDA) Church is a Protestant denomination with approximately 15 million members worldwide. The Branch Davidians were a splinter group of the SDA church, founded by Victor Houteff, a Bulgarian immigrant. Houteff was kicked out of the SDA in 1929 for criticizing the church's leaders. Five years later, he established his sect, which he named the Davidian Seventh Day Adventist Association. He chose the name to suggest that during the Second Coming, the Messiah would occupy the throne of the Hebrew King David. Years later, Houteff's sect split into factions, one of which became the Branch Davidians. In biblical terms, *branch* is regarded as a reference to the coming of the Messiah.

David Koresh was born Vernon Wayne Howell in Houston, Texas, in 1959. After taking over the Branch Davidians, Howell changed his name to David Koresh. He chose his first name after the Hebrew King David. The name *Koresh* is Hebrew for Cyrus, a sixth-century BCE Persian king who permitted the Jews to return to Israel. Many Christians believe that Jesus will not return to Earth until the Jews have established their homeland in Israel. By taking the name David Koresh, he sought to encourage that belief among his followers.

showed up with a warrant to conduct a search, a firefight broke out, in which six Davidians and four agents died.

Thus began the 51-day siege, which ended when federal agents shot tear-gas canisters into the compound. Fires erupted in the buildings. The flames spread quickly, and dozens of Davidians were killed. When agents picked through the rubble, they found that many of the Davidians, including Koresh, had died of single gunshot wounds to their heads. The Davidians had taken their own lives.

The siege at Waco resulted in the deaths of nearly 80 Branch Davidians, including 29 children. Did the federal agents go too far? Federal agents acted with the intention of protecting children and others who lived inside the compound. Nonetheless, the siege raised questions about whether the government acted properly. Critics have argued that the weapons stockpiled at the compound were obtained legally and that the Second Amendment to the Constitution allows citizens the right to own guns. This would include the Davidians. Critics also asserted that there was no proof that children had been abused. Rhys H. Williams, associate professor of sociology at Southern Illinois University, said:

While there is no easy or clear answer as to whether the Branch Davidians were illegally persecuted by the government, there are still questions as to whether the state should have intervened. . . . In retrospect, perhaps the only real surprise of the Waco conflagration is that the government confronted an apocalyptic communalist group led by a charismatic leader with paranoiac tendencies and a $200,000 arsenal—and was then "surprised" that it ended violently.[1]

Though the siege is still debated, others have contended that the government acted correctly in attempting to protect the minors within the compound. Investigator Joyce Sparks had noted significant evidence of abuse in the months leading up to the raid.

MILITIA MOVEMENT

The siege in Waco had a lasting impact. It helped encourage a new wave of extremism in the United States—the so-called militia movement. Members of militia groups fear that the U.S. government has made secret plans to deny citizens their rights. In some cases, citing the experience of Waco, militia groups have advocated armed resistance against the federal government.

The militia movement had its origins in the tax-protest movements of the 1970s. Its members were people who, on ill-conceived grounds, refused to pay their federal income taxes. After a wave of prosecutions by the Internal Revenue Service, many of the tax-protest groups united into organizations that took a dim view of federal authority of any kind.

A number of militias formed, including the Michigan Militia and the Republic of Texas Militia. Other groups, such as the Montana Freemen and Posse Comitatus, declared themselves as sovereign organizations not bound by the concepts of U.S. laws that were not specifically included in the Constitution. Members harbored racist ideologies as well as a deep distrust of the government. They developed conspiracy theories and accused the government of taking

Posse Comitatus

Posse Comitatus was a loosely organized association of antigovernment activists. The group drew its name from the U.S. Posse Comitatus Act of 1878, which prohibits the use of federal troops as local law enforcement officers. *Posse comitatus* means "power of the county" in Latin.

The founder of the group, Henry Beach, declared that only laws specifically contained in the Constitution can be enforced. In other words, he suggested all the laws passed by Congress and the state legislatures could not be enforced.

The movement grew out of the tax protests of the 1970s. When the Internal Revenue Service began prosecuting tax resisters, groups such as Posse Comitatus formed. They urged their members to arm themselves to resist government intrusion in their lives. During the 1980s, several violent clashes with authorities led to the breakup of Posse Comitatus.

elaborate measures to eavesdrop on citizens. They claimed the U.S. government had secret plans to confiscate their guns, build concentration camps, and take over the world. They believed that secret codes had been etched into street signs to direct the enemy troops once civil unrest broke out.

Some individuals have created such violence and destruction on behalf of their beliefs that they would seem to be part of a larger group. While serving in the army, Terry Nichols met Timothy McVeigh, a young man from a suburb of Buffalo, New York. The two men shared views about the evil intentions of the government. During the siege at Waco, McVeigh traveled to the Texas city in support of the Branch Davidians. McVeigh told a local reporter during the siege, "The government is continually growing bigger and more powerful, and the people need to prepare to defend themselves against government control."[2]

McVeigh was so troubled by the siege that he and Nichols made plans to send a message to the federal government. The men bombed the Alfred P. Murrah Federal Building in Oklahoma City, Oklahoma, on April 19, 1995. Nichols and McVeigh sent their message to the government, taking 168 lives.

Rescue workers search for victims after the bombing of the Alfred P. Murrah Federal Building in Oklahoma City, Oklahoma.

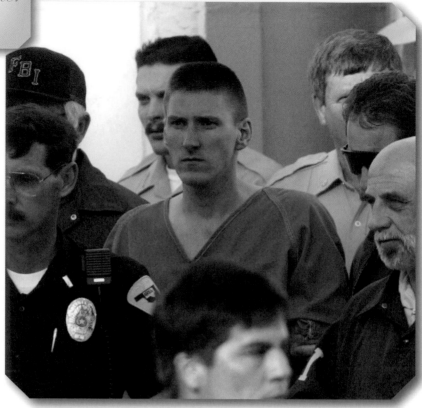

Timothy McVeigh, who was found guilty of bombing the Alfred P. Murrah Federal Building, was influenced by The Turner Diaries.

SPREADING THE EXTREMIST MESSAGE

The First Amendment guarantees the freedom of the press. Extremist groups have made use of printing presses, radio, television, and, more recently, the Internet. At times, however, the groups have faced constraints on their rights to publish and broadcast their messages.

In 1917, Postmaster General Albert S. Burleson refused to deliver copies of *The Masses*, a socialist literary magazine. Burleson contended that the magazine, and other publications critical of the government, violated the Espionage Act. He claimed that their opposition to U.S. involvement in World War I was illegal. The publisher of *The Masses* won a court order from U.S. Judge Leonard Hand directing Burleson's mail carriers to deliver the magazine. Dissent during time of war, Hand wrote, is "a hard-bought acquisition in the fight for freedom."[1] However, an appeals court overturned Hand's order. The socialist press was silenced for the duration of the war, despite its nonviolent dissent.

In 1927, an anti-Semitic and antiblack publisher, Jay M. Near, was sued by the Minnesota attorney general, who sought to silence Near's newspaper. A local judge barred Near from continuing publication of the *Saturday Press*. The case entered the court system. In 1931, the Supreme Court ruled in Near's favor. It ordered that the government could not exercise prior restraint over the press. In other words, the government could not shut down a newspaper because its message was offensive to some. The Supreme Court cleared the way for the *Saturday Press* to publish its articles essentially free of government censorship.

FREEDOM OF SPEECH AMONG
POLITICAL DISSIDENTS

The decision in the Near case helped the communist newspaper *Daily Worker* spread its political message. This daily newspaper was first published by the Communist Party in 1924. By 1958, the party was forced to cut back to a weekly publication. Also, by this time, human rights abuses in the Soviet Union, a communist country, had become well-known. This prompted many U.S. communists to question the ideology and abandon the movement. In later years, U.S. communists tried to revive a daily paper but were met with mixed success. In 1968, a new daily communist paper, the *Daily World*, began publication. It continued until 1991 when the newspaper, then known as the *People's Weekly World*, printed its last edition. Currently, Communist Party USA maintains a weekly newspaper.

As communists found themselves losing support, other extremists discovered the media could provide

them with effective outlets for their messages. From
1967 until 1980, the Black Panther Party published
the *Black Panther*, a weekly paper that promoted the
group's ideology. Black Panther leaders established
the paper because they believed their activities
were not covered fairly by the mainstream press.
They were concerned that the media distorted
their message and did not report enough on their
community activism.

Other groups, such as George Lincoln Rockwell's
American Nazi Party, published newspapers as
well. Many local chapters of the Ku Klux Klan
published sporadically. Most of these publications
were available through underground sources only.
Newsstands and bookstores generally did not carry
Klan books and newspapers on their racks.

THE TURNER DIARIES

One extremist novel, *The Turner Diaries,* did
become an underground phenomenon. It was
written in 1978 by William Pierce, an organizer of
the National Alliance, a neo-Nazi group started in
West Virginia. In *The Turner Diaries,* worldwide chaos
results in a nuclear holocaust. From the rubble, a
superior Aryan (white) race rises. White survivors

resolve to rid their society of "undesirables" such as Jews, African Americans, Hispanics—and even white women married to them. The main character, Earl Turner, describes the lynching of thousands of women:

William Pierce

William Pierce, author of *The Turner Diaries*, was a physics professor at Oregon State University before becoming a prominent figure in the extremist movement. Pierce joined George Lincoln Rockwell's American Nazi Party. After Rockwell's death in 1967, Pierce founded his own group, the National Alliance. In 1978, he published *The Turner Diaries* under the pseudonym Andrew Macdonald.

Oklahoma City bomber Timothy McVeigh has not been the only extremist influenced by the dark messages of *The Turner Diaries*. In 1985, members of a neo-Nazi group known as the Order were charged with the murder of prominent Jewish talk-show host Alan Berg. A witness at the trial testified that members of the Order were devoted readers of Pierce's book. "You should read it, partner, it's all there," the witness said. "Everything that's going to happen is in *The Turner Diaries*."[3]

Pierce died in 2002. At the time of his death, the National Alliance was believed to have had an annual income of $1 million. This sum was earned through the sales of Pierce's books and a record label that sells music inspired by extremist messages.

At practically every street corner I passed this evening . . . there was a dangling corpse, four at every intersection. . . . About a mile from here is a group of about thirty, each with an identical placard around its neck bearing the printed legend, "I betrayed my race."[2]

More than 500,000 copies of the book have been printed. Timothy McVeigh read the novel several

times. He may have based the 1995 Oklahoma City
bombing on a scenario from the book. Despite its
racist message, and its supposed role in the deaths
of the Oklahoma City victims, the U.S. government
has not attempted to censor it. The days when the
government believed it could censor the written
words of extremists ended with the 1931 Supreme
Court decision that allowed the publication of the
Saturday Press.

OVER THE AIRWAVES

While the printed word cannot be censored,
broadcast messages may not be as protected. In 1988,
the city council of Kansas City, Missouri, attempted
to censor the cable television broadcast of a racist
series titled *Race and Reason*. Beginning in 1984, this
series was produced by California Ku Klux Klan
leader Tom Metzger. To stop the broadcast, the city
council voted to end the city's public access cable
channel. This channel had specifically been set up
to provide citizens with airtime on cable television.
Representing the Klan, the ACLU sued the city to
prevent the council's vote from going into effect. A
year later, the council settled the lawsuit by voting
to restore the public-access channel. "If there is

Resistance Music

Some extremist groups have started their own record labels to produce what they call "Resistance Music." The music features malicious, racist lyrics and is usually sold on Web sites maintained by groups such as the late William Pierce's National Alliance. As one British newspaper columnist said, "It's awful stuff, musically and morally, but it creates dilemmas for liberal America. They have given their imprimatur to rap music. . . . What is the difference between Pierce's 'Resistance' and Ice Cube's regular declarations of war on the Los Angeles (Police) Department?"[6]

a victory today, it is a victory for the First Amendment," said Dick Kurtenbach, a Missouri ACLU leader.[4]

Extremist groups also use the Internet to spread their messages of hate. The Stormfront White Nationalist Community, a white supremacist group, has a popular Web site. The racist site hosts a discussion group with more than 1,500 hits each weekday. Such a site would be banned in other countries. But under the First Amendment, it is protected. Extremist organizers in the United States are aware of their unique privilege to export their messages to like-minded people. As Stormfront spokesman Jamie Kelso stated,

> No other country has a First Amendment. In Canada, where we're very big, you can be jailed for what's called hate speech. You can be jailed and fined and sanctioned. Same thing in Germany.[5]

The Teardown band performs at a memorial concert for George Lincoln Rockwell, who founded the American Nazi Party.

Abortion and pro-choice advocates and protestors express their views outside the U.S. Supreme Court on December 8, 1993.

ABORTION OPPOSITION

The U.S. Supreme Court handed down the *Roe v. Wade* decision in 1973. This decision granted women the fundamental right to seek abortions in the United States. Opponents of abortion rights immediately searched for ways to sidestep the ruling and deny abortions to women.

Many antiabortion rights activists sought to change abortion laws through court challenges and by lobbying government representatives. However, other opponents formed organized groups and vowed to take their opposition to the streets.

Operation Rescue

By the mid-1980s, several antiabortion groups operated in the United States. Among the most influential was Operation Rescue, organized by Randall Terry of Binghamton, New York. Operation Rescue activists protested at the doors of abortion clinics. They employed a variety of tactics. They often harassed staff members and prevented them and clients from entering the buildings. They waved photographs of aborted fetuses. Considering themselves "sidewalk counselors," they approached women as they entered the clinics and urged them to seek alternatives to abortion, such as adoption.

In 1991, Operation Rescue targeted abortion clinics in Wichita, Kansas. For 46 days, activists harassed physicians, clinic staff members, and clients. A federal judge in Kansas issued a court order barring the Operation Rescue activists from blocking the entrances to abortion clinics. The

Harassment

Nearly two decades after the abortion clinic protests in Wichita, Kansas, Operation Rescue continues to harass clinic workers. Officials of Operation Rescue acknowledge that they rummage through the trash at employees' homes in search of incriminating evidence. They also follow staff members around town, picket them at restaurants, and hurl insults at them in public. According to Operation Rescue President Troy Newman, "I want these employees to realize that their lives have changed. As long as they're embedded in the abortion industry receiving blood money, they can't live a normal life."[2]

judge based the decision on an 1871 law prohibiting harassment of freed slaves. Still, many Operation Rescue activists ignored the court order. By the end of summer, police had made some 2,700 arrests. Terry stated, "When government officials see people peacefully blockading abortion mills, they begin to take them seriously."[1]

PROTESTS TURN VIOLENT

The activities of antiabortion extremists have raised significant constitutional questions. The activists maintain that their rights to free speech and assembly must be respected. Supporters contend that they have the right to take their protests to the doors of abortion clinics.

However, *Roe v. Wade* established the right of women to seek abortions. With the *Roe* decision, the Supreme Court specifically noted that the Ninth and Fourteenth Amendments to the Constitution guarantee the right to privacy. And this right to privacy extends to decisions made by women who seek abortions.

Not to be deterred, some antiabortion activists became extreme in their actions, turning to threats and violence. They bombed abortion clinics in a number of cities—always at night and when they believed the clinics were empty. But in 1993 and 1994, two abortion clinic physicians and a bodyguard were murdered in Pensacola, Florida. This prompted Congress to adopt the Freedom of Access to Clinic Entrances Act, establishing stiff fines and even jail time for people who block the entrances to abortion clinics.

In 1993, Colorado adopted

Guilty of Murder

Michael Griffin, a factory worker, had participated in several protests outside abortion clinics in Pensacola, Florida. He was charged with murdering physician David Gunn outside a clinic on March 5, 1993. Police said Griffin waited for the doctor to leave the clinic and shot him in the back of the head. Griffin immediately dropped his gun, approached a nearby police officer, and confessed to the crime. Griffin was convicted and sentenced to life in prison.

A year later, Paul Hill, a former minister, approached physician John Britton as he arrived at a Pensacola clinic. Using a shotgun, Hill murdered Britton and his bodyguard, James Barrett. He also wounded Barrett's wife, June. During his trial, Hill confessed to the shootings but expressed no remorse. A jury deliberated just 20 minutes before convicting Hill. He was executed in 2003.

a law that required protesters to remain at least 100 feet (30 m) away from abortion clinic entrances. In 2000, the Supreme Court upheld the law, arguing that the statute did not violate the rights of abortion activists to free speech. The law did place reasonable restrictions on the activities of protesters while also maintaining the clients' rights to privacy. Since the Supreme Court ruling, other states have passed similar laws.

Despite such laws, violence has continued to be a part of the antiabortion rights movement. The National Abortion Rights Action League-Pro Choice America Foundation (NARAL-Pro Choice America) is the nation's leading abortion rights group. According to this foundation, four people have been murdered in abortion clinic-related cases since the two incidents in Pensacola, Florida. Abortion clients and clinic staff members have endured numerous bomb threats, vandalism, and other violent acts.

Bombings and Arsons

NARAL-Pro Choice America has tracked violent actions by antiabortion activists that occurred between 1977 and 2004 in the United States. According to the group, these incidents include more than 40 bombings, 170 arsons, 80 attempted bombings and arsons, and nearly 600 bomb threats against abortion clinics.

Another scare tactic employed by activists is to mail letters to abortion clinics claiming the letters contain the deadly anthrax bacteria. NARAL-Pro Choice America says more than 250 clinics in America have received letters threatening anthrax contamination since 2001.

DIVISION WITHIN THE MOVEMENT

Abortion opponents have denounced the laws passed by Congress as well as laws passed in Colorado and other states. Because the laws keep them from picketing near clinic doors, protestors resort to shouting at staff members or patients from a distance. The activists contend that these techniques have proven ineffective. Some abortion opponents believe physical confrontation is the only tactic that works. Teresa Lindley, an antiabortion rights activist, was arrested for blocking the entrance of a Pensacola clinic. She stated, "Bombing is the only thing left if the other things don't work. . . ."[3]

There are differences of opinions even within the extreme fringes of the antiabortion movement. Many abortion protesters believe that violence is not the answer and that protests should be conducted peacefully within the law. Joseph Scheidler is the director of the Pro-Life Action Network. He points out that bombing clinics is not a tactic that prevents abortions. The clients of destroyed clinics still found access to abortions elsewhere. Furthermore, each destroyed clinic was eventually rebuilt. Scheidler added that the activists responsible for violent acts were invariably caught and sentenced to lengthy prison terms. Scheidler stated:

> What lasting advantage is there to show for the actions they were accused of? The damaged clinics have reopened or have sent their clients elsewhere. While we understand the feelings of anger, outrage, and frustration, . . . we advise pro-lifers not to resort to violent tactics, but to save lives and stop abortions through nonviolent, direct action. [4]

Truth Truck

Barred from effectively blocking the entrances of abortion clinics, groups such as Operation Rescue have looked for new ways to deliver their messages. Operation Rescue utilizes its Truth Truck, which drives through communities displaying photos of aborted fetuses. In late 2007, police in Georgia arrested the driver of the Truth Truck. Robert Dean Roethlisberger Jr. was charged with breaking a public decency law by displaying obscene images. However, the charges were dropped. Attorneys for Operation Rescue argued that by driving the Truth Truck, Roethlisberger was exercising his First Amendment right to free expression.

Terry Randall originally organized Operation Rescue. He has since founded Loyal Opposition and continues to oppose abortion.

Animal rights activists peacefully protest a primate research center in Massachusetts.

PROTECTING THE PLANET

ules Rosenbaum is a highly regarded physician at the University of California at Los Angeles, where he searches for cures to eye disease. In August 2007, Rosenbaum found a curious package under his car. The police determined the package was a crude homemade bomb. They did not need to conduct an extensive investigation to find the culprit. Three days after the bomb was discovered, an extremist group calling itself the Animal Liberation Brigade took responsibility for the attempt to kill Rosenbaum. The group stated its reasons very clearly in a message released to reporters:

> *He and his wife . . . are the target of rebellion for the vile and evil things he does to primates at UCLA . . . torture on fully conscious primates in his lab. We have heard their whimpers and screeches of pain. . . . We have seen hell and it is in Rosenbaum's lab.*[1]

There is no question that Rosenbaum and many other research scientists experiment on live animals such as monkeys, mice, and rats. Sometimes, the animals are harmed or even killed during the experiments. However, scientists justify their actions by the advancements in medicine that have been achieved through experimentation on animals. They argue that human lives have been saved from diseases and disabilities because new drugs, surgical techniques, and procedures were first tried on animals.

In March 2008, a California judge signed a court order protecting scientists at all ten of the University of California campuses from attacks by three ecoterrorist groups. This included the UCLA Primate Freedom, the Animal Liberation Brigade, and the Animal Liberation Front. The university sought the order after six masked people tried to force their way into the home of one of its scientists. Allegedly, the activists assaulted the scientist's husband when he confronted them in the doorway.

Ecoterrorists insist that animals have rights and vow to put an end to research that places any living thing in jeopardy. These extremists have been very open about their intentions. Some have defended killing humans as a strategy for ending invasive experimentation, known as vivisection, on animals. In 2005, California surgeon Jerry Vlasak, a leader of the Animal Liberation Front, testified before the U.S. Senate. He told lawmakers that the murder of research scientists would provide an effective means of halting such experiments. "I don't think you'd have to kill—assassinate—too many [humans]," Vlasak said. "I think for five lives, ten lives, fifteen lives, we could save a million, 2 million or 10 million nonhuman lives."[2]

Roots of the Movement

While the animal rights movement dates to the nineteenth century, the radical animal rights movement traces its roots to the 1960s. A group of British activists formed the Hunt Saboteurs Association (HSA) to disrupt the sport of fox hunting. HSA radicals blocked roads and harassed hunters. They used chemical sprays to throw the hunters' dogs off the scents.

Activists employed radical tactics elsewhere as well. Ronnie Lee and Cliff Goodman were members of the animal rights group Band of Mercy. In 1972, they were jailed for setting fire to a research center in England that was known to use vivisection and experiment on animals. When Lee was released from prison in 1976, he reorganized Band of Mercy into the Animal Liberation Front (ALF).

The ALF soon formed chapters in the United States. In 1979, members broke into a lab at the New York University Medical School and released five animals. Elsewhere, dozens of other activists took

Commitment to Research

A 2000 California law specifically permits the use of animals for medical research, but the law states that for all other purposes, scientists must use research techniques that do not rely on animals. According to the Chicago-based National Anti-Vivisection Society, this component of the law was aimed at the cosmetics industry. For many years the cosmetic industry tested new products on animals, often with harmful results.

similar measures. They did not cause personal injury or extensive property damage, but they disrupted experiments and harassed scientists.

The activities escalated, however, and some of the incidents could not be classified as minor. In 1987, radicals firebombed research labs at the University of California-Davis and Michigan State University. Each lab sustained millions of dollars in damage. In the Michigan case, activist Rod Coronado was convicted and sentenced to three years in prison. After his conviction, Coronado said that he had no regrets.

By 1993, the U.S. Agriculture Department and the U.S. Justice Department reported that animal rights activists had committed more than 300 break-ins, vandalisms, arsons, and thefts since the New York University incident.

Extreme Measures

As pollution, climate change, overdevelopment, and other environmental concerns grew, radical groups formed to take matters into their own hands. Established in 1980, Earth First! was one of the earliest radical environmental groups. Originally, these activists practiced nonviolent civil disobedience. They often tied themselves to trees, blocking builders from clearing wooded areas for construction. Next, they turned to sabotage, such as disabling construction equipment. For many radicals, however, the techniques advocated by Earth First! were far too mild. They called for more dramatic methods.

In 1992, radical environmental activists formed the Earth Liberation Front (ELF). These activists have attacked hundreds of facilities they deem to be threats to the environment. In 2003, the most expensive case of ecoterrorism was committed in San Diego, California. Arsonists burned down a housing development under construction and caused

SUVs Under Attack

Due to the amount of gasoline they use, sport utility vehicles, or SUVs, have emerged as targets of the ecoterrorist movement. In August 2003, ecoterrorists set fire to more than 40 Hummers and other SUVs at an auto dealership in West Covina, California. This caused more than $2 million in damage.

On the same night as the West Covina fire, vandals struck auto dealerships in the nearby California communities of Arcadia and Duarte, damaging several SUVs. In Monrovia, an SUV parked on a street was damaged. Scrawled across the vehicle was "ELF," the initials of Earth Liberation Front.

SUVs have been targeted elsewhere as well. At a dealership in Erie, Pennsylvania, three SUVs were set on fire in January 2003. In this incident, the ELF activists left a message. They wrote that that the SUVs have been targeted "to remove the profit motive from the killing of the natural environment."[3]

approximately $50 million in damage. Taking responsibility for the crime, ELF activists strung a banner across the charred site: "If you build it, we will burn it."[4]

In 2005, federal agents arrested ten radical environmental activists and charged them with a string of crimes in five states. The crimes included committing vandalism and arson at timber companies, meatpacking plants, a car dealership, and a ski resort. "This was a classic case of terrorism, despite their protests of lofty humane goals," said U.S. Attorney Stephen Peifer, who prosecuted the activists. "It was pure luck no one was killed or injured by their actions."[5]

Radical environmental activists justify their extreme actions by arguing that Earth is in crisis, and environmental protection laws have proven ineffective. They contend that drastic strategies are necessary to protect Earth.

The Earth Liberation Front may have set fires that destroyed two newly
constructed homes and damaged a third near Snohomish, Washington.

American Muslims pray outside the Federal Courthouse in Virginia as nine members of the Virginia Jihad Network were on trial.

JIHADISTS IN THE
UNITED STATES

On September 11, 2001, terrorists attacked the World Trade Center in New York City and the Pentagon in Washington DC. In the months following the attack, a group of 11 men often gathered quietly in the woods of the Virginia countryside. They did so, they claimed, to play paintball games. According to federal prosecutors, however, this was no ordinary group of paintball enthusiasts. Rather, the men were practicing military techniques that they planned to use in attacks on the United States. Unlike the 9/11 terrorists, all of whom came from Arab nations, these 11 members of the so-called Virginia Jihad Network were U.S. citizens.

Nine of the men eventually received jail terms for plotting terrorist acts. Two men were acquitted. Following the 2006 sentencing, prosecutors proclaimed that they had broken up the most significant jihadist plot on U.S. soil since the 2001 attacks. A federal law enforcement official told the *Washington Post*:

> A cadre of people . . . had gone overseas and obtained training from violent jihadist groups whose primary ideology is hatred of the United States. They were walking around the national capital area with training in small arms, infantry tactics, any number of skills that could be used to mount a strike.[1]

BEYOND THE PATRIOT ACT

The Virginia Jihad Network was broken by federal agents using a provision of the USA Patriot Act. The provision enabled the Central Intelligence Agency (CIA) to share information with the Federal Bureau of Investigation (FBI) and other federal and local law enforcement agencies. Prior to the adoption of the Patriot Act, the CIA's role was regarded as an intelligence-gathering agency whose information would be used for diplomatic purposes, among other intelligence roles. Under the Patriot Act, the CIA could now share its files on suspected terrorists with foreign connections with the FBI and police. In the case of the Virginia Jihad Network, the CIA had developed

What Is Jihad?

Jihad is an Arabic term that means "holy struggle," and a *mujahid* means the "participant in a jihad." Over the years, jihad has been applied to the struggle of Muslim fundamentalists to spread their faith. In the Qur'an, Islam's holy book, the term *jihad fi sabil illah* describes warfare against enemies of the Muslim community. The term has often been invoked by Islamic leaders who threaten to use violence against non-Muslims.

Not all Muslims embrace the extremists' holy war jihad. According to many Islamic scholars, radicals have misinterpreted the meaning of jihad. They argue that the Prophet Mohammad, the founder of Islam, taught that "the greatest jihad is the one a person carries out against his lower soul."[2] This means that jihad is a constant struggle to resist sin. Many Muslims also insist that theirs is a pacifist faith and that that Allah, the Arabic word for God, abhors violence. Pacifist Muslims point out that the Qur'an teaches, "Each time they kindle the fire of war, Allah extinguishes it. They rush about the earth corrupting it. Allah does not love corrupters."[3]

evidence suggesting the jihadists were receiving support from radicals in other countries.

The "information sharing" component of the law has been welcomed by law enforcement agencies. However, the law contains other controversial provisions that allow the government to perform eavesdropping and other secretive measures without a court order, or a warrant, in order to gather evidence on suspected terrorists. Government intelligence-gathering agencies can now share information.

Adopted in the days following the 2001 terror attacks, the Patriot Act has been criticized by those who believe it compromises basic constitutional rights. Supporters argue that when it comes to rooting out terrorists, all methods are justified. Former federal prosecutor Andrew McBride stated:

> We're arresting people for talking about things, thinking about things, training for things. I think you will see more of it as the government moves from a traditional criminal law model of post-event reaction to pre-event interdiction. But that's where the civil liberties rubber meets the road.[4]

In the case of the Virginia Jihad Network, charges arose that suggested federal agents went beyond the provisions of the Patriot Act. One of the men acquitted in the case was Sabri Ben Kahla. He was arrested at a university in Saudi Arabia and brought back to the United States. He was held in a prison for a month before being charged as a member of the Virginia cell. Shortly after he was found not guilty, he said, "This is not the America I know. Maybe this is what Jewish people felt with the Nazis and people in Russia experienced under Stalin."[5]

U.S. Targets

Over the years, radical Muslims have found many reasons to hate the United States. Many radicalists and others disagree with some of the governments that the United States chooses to support. In 1979, radical students staged a siege of the U.S. Embassy in Tehran, Iran, mainly because the United States had supported Shah Mohammad Reza Pahlavi, who had recently been deposed in a revolution prompted by Islamic clerics. Many Muslims harbor animosity toward the United States for its support of Israel, which has defended itself against Arab aggression and has been unable to come to terms with Palestinian leaders on establishing a homeland for the Palestinian people.

In 1991, the U.S. military sparked the anger of radical Muslims when it used bases in Saudi Arabia to launch an attack on Iraq during Operation Desert Storm. Radical Muslims believe the use of holy, Saudi land by non-Muslims is an affront to their religion.

The U.S. public became aware of jihadism in 1993 when a group of jihadists based in New Jersey detonated a bomb in the parking garage beneath the World Trade Center. Suddenly, U.S. citizens were very aware of the hatred harbored against them by radical Islamic fundamentalists.

Unlike the 2001 attacks, in which hijacked airliners were flown into the Twin Towers, the 1993 attack was not a suicide mission. A cell of Islamic extremists planted a bomb in a truck that exploded in the World Trade Center's underground garage. Six people were killed and more than 1,000 were injured as the massive building shook on its foundation. Fortunately, the building did not topple into nearby New York skyscrapers. Such a disaster could have resulted in as many as 250,000 deaths. Sifting through the rubble, police found the vehicle registration number on the frame of the truck. This led them to the rental agency that leased the vehicle to the jihadists. Nine conspirators were convicted and sentenced to lengthy prison terms.

Since then, aggressive law-enforcement tactics have uncovered other Islamic extremist groups operating in the United States. In most cases, authorities have employed methods available to them under the Patriot Act. These methods include sharing information between government agencies and monitoring the use of personal computers by tracking Internet usage and e-mails.

For example, thanks to interagency cooperation, agents were able to use information gained by wiretapping José Padilla. Federal agents pursued evidence suggesting Padilla intended to explode a "dirty bomb" in a major U.S. city. A dirty bomb is composed of nuclear materials collected from hospitals or construction sites. It is less devastating than an actual nuclear bomb. When exploded, the bomb would cause relatively minor damage. But its poisonous contents could spread in the atmosphere and potentially kill hundreds of people. In 2002, Padilla and two others were arrested. In 2007, Padilla was convicted in a separate case by a federal court. He was found guilty of charges that he planned to support jihadists in other countries.

An artist's courtroom sketch of the six men accused of plotting an attack on the Fort Dix Army base

Also in 2007, federal agents arrested six members of a radical Islamic cell. These men were charged with plotting a military-style assault on Fort Dix in New Jersey. The conspirators hoped to shoot their way into the fort and kill as many soldiers as possible before retreating. "Today, we dodged a bullet," said Jody Weiss, the Philadelphia FBI agent who announced the arrests.[6]

HARMLESS ACTIVITY

The ACLU and other civil libertarian groups have denounced the Patriot Act. They object to

The Fort Dix Six

Six men were charged with planning to murder U.S. soldiers at Fort Dix, New Jersey, in 2007. They were alleged to have formed a terror cell in the Philadelphia-New Jersey area. Only one, Jordanian-born Mohamad Shnewer, is a U.S. citizen. Four are ethnic Albanians (from the former Yugoslavia) who settled in the United States. The other conspirator immigrated to the United States from Turkey.

There was no direct evidence to link the six men to al-Qaeda or other terrorist organizations. However, according to court records they were prepared to carry out their plan and die "in the name of Allah."[8]

the fact that the law allows federal agents to eavesdrop on innocent people. Under the Patriot Act, federal agents often do not have to obtain a warrant to wiretap phones, search homes, or otherwise spy on people. Civil libertarians argue that when police must obtain a judge's permission to perform surveillance, the court provides a measure of oversight. Many believe warrants serve a crucial function that is disregarded under the Patriot Act. ACLU director Laura Murphy states:

> *In general, this law limits the role of the federal judiciary. The police can now come into your home, download information off of your computer, go through your personal possessions, and you'll never know they were there.*[7]

Law enforcement officials and civil libertarians may debate the benefits of the Patriot Act and other investigatory techniques. Meanwhile, many law-abiding U.S. Muslims feel that they have been targeted since 2001 and have become the victims of prejudice because of the activities of a handful of terrorists.

According to the Council on American-Islamic Relations, some 1,500 cases of abuse toward Muslim Americans have occurred annually since 9/11. The international Islamic terrorist group al-Qaeda and its leader Osama bin Laden have taken credit for the 2001 attacks as well as many other terrorist attacks around the world. However, the council insists that al-Qaeda does not represent the vast majority of Muslims. Sayed Moustafa Al-Qazwini, a religious leader of the Islamic Education Center of Orange County, California, stated:

> Al-Qaeda does not represent the true Islam. Unfortunately, a group of misled people are following a mass murderer by the name of Osama bin Laden and they do not represent the Islamic culture or the Arabic culture.[9]

One of the attorneys of the Virginia jihadists argued that the group drew interest from federal agents simply because they were Muslim. Attorney John K. Zwerling argued that the defendants did

Is the Patriot Act Working?

In 2005, President George W. Bush delivered a speech in which he claimed the USA Patriot Act had resulted in the arrests of more than 400 suspects in terrorism cases. An analysis by Syracuse University concluded, however, that most of the cases involved minor criminals who were not involved in terror-related activities. The ACLU has sought to abolish the Patriot Act. The ACLU has stated, "The president's Patriot Act rhetoric simply doesn't match the facts. The American people deserve an honest debate, not rehashed photo opportunities full of inaccuracies designed to mislead."[11]

nothing more than play paintball in the woods—a harmless activity that should not have raised suspicions. Zwerling said, "There is no way this [case] would have been prosecuted if these young men weren't Muslims."[10]

PROTECTING THE
HOMELAND

*President Bush signs the USA Patriot Terrorism
Reauthorization Act of 2005.*

*The National Socialist Movement (NSM) rallies in South Carolina
against immigration.*

New Sparks to Extremism

In 2007, an estimated 12 million
illegal immigrants, mostly Latinos,
lived in the United States. The number of illegal
immigrants entering the United States each year
raises concerns that they will take jobs from U.S.

citizens, overburden social services, and commit crimes. Politicians cannot agree on how to curb the problem.

The intense debate over immigration in the United States has sparked a new chapter in extremist activity. The Southern Poverty Law Center (SPLC), an Alabama-based organization, investigates extremist activity in the United States. According to the SPLC, the number of extremist groups operating in the United States grew by one-third between 2000 and 2005. They credit this increase to the rise in anti-immigrant extremist groups, such as the Ku Klux Klan.

Membership in the Ku Klux Klan has increased during recent years. The approximate number of groups has increased from 90 to 150. "If any one single issue or trend can be credited with re-energizing the Klan, it is the debate over immigration in America," said Deborah M. Lauter, civil rights director of the Anti-Defamation League.[1] Historically speaking, a large driver in the Klan's rise during the 1920s was a similar anti-immigration sentiment.

Another extremist group that has grown during the immigration debate is the National Socialist

Movement (NSM), or neo-Nazis. Its members wear replicas of World War II-era Nazi uniforms, complete with swastikas. The group has been politically active in Washington. In 2008, it supported John Taylor Bowles, a former U.S. Agriculture Department bureaucrat, as a presidential candidate. Bowles, who has gone on to organize his own extremist group (the National Socialist Order of America), has made illegal immigration a centerpiece of his platform. Campaigning in full Nazi regalia, Bowles said, "I'm going to

---

Extremist Candidates

John Taylor Bowles, the National Socialist Order of America's candidate for president in 2008, was not the first dissident candidate to run in a mainstream political race. Socialist Party candidates have a history of competing in U.S. elections, despite the party's minority status among more favored political beliefs.

In 1912, Eugene Debs won 6 percent of the popular vote as a candidate for president. Debs and other socialist leaders made several other runs for president throughout the twentieth century, none of which seriously challenged the Republican or Democratic candidates.

In 1965, American Nazi Party founder George Lincoln Rockwell ran for governor of Virginia. He received less than 6,000 votes out of more than 560,000 votes.

Gus Hall ran four times for president as the candidate of the Communist Party USA. In his 1980 and 1984 campaigns, the vice presidential candidate on Hall's ticket was Angela Davis. She is a former member of the Black Panther Party and one of the most renowned radicals of the 1960s. In both elections, Hall and Davis raised little interest among voters. In 1984, for example, the pair received an approximate 36,000 votes out of more than 90 million.

move large segments of the nonwhite population back to their respective homelands because I have a right to do that by law and I'll probably declare it a national emergency."[2]

A COMPLEX ISSUE

The growth of the Ku Klux Klan and NSM illustrates how some groups can attract followers by offering simple answers to complex issues. And few issues are as complex as immigration. Political leaders have endorsed a wide variety of solutions but have failed to win a consensus in Congress.

Some of the proposed policies would welcome Latinos and others into the country. These solutions include a guest-worker program that would allow illegal immigrants to stay in the country and hold jobs. The path to a citizenship program would enable illegal immigrants to apply for citizenship after working in the United States for several years. Some proposed solutions are more rigid. Political leaders have endorsed stiff penalties on employers who knowingly hire illegal immigrants. Others want to heighten security on the U.S.-Mexico border and arrest immigrants as they attempt to cross into the United States.

None of these solutions are acceptable to extremist leaders. Jeff Schoep, commander of the NSM, suggested a radically different solution. He proposed recalling tens of thousands of U.S. troops from Iraq and stationing them along the Mexican border. These troops would create a barrier that no illegal immigrant could pass through.

In April 2007, approximately 80 members of the NSM staged an anti-immigration rally on the steps of the state capitol in Columbia, South Carolina. "A lot of them [immigrants] don't speak English," Schoep said. "They're trying not to speak English. They're coming to conquer our country, not become a part of it."[3] Approximately 150 onlookers attended the rally. Many heckled the neo-Nazis as they voiced their racist messages. Approximately 200 state troopers made sure the two sides were kept apart. The extremists were able to exercise their rights to free speech.

Opponents of the Ku Klux Klan and the NSM suggest that extremists offer quick, easy, and inhumane solutions. They believe the extremists are not driven by the economic or social consequences of illegal immigration, but by bigotry against nonwhites.

DEFINE AND STRENGTHEN FREEDOMS

Extremism has been a part of U.S. society since the eighteenth century when John Fries and his followers harassed tax collectors over tax reforms. For many extremist groups, the results of their actions justify the oftentimes violent or illegal methods. Regardless of who "wins" or "loses" in these situations, the controversy over extremism has helped the U.S. system of justice define and strengthen the freedoms that all U.S. citizens enjoy.

In 1931, the U.S. Supreme Court ruled that the government could not exercise prior restraint by prohibiting what Jay M. Near's anti-Semitic and antiblack *Saturday Press* may print. Four decades later, the *Saturday Press* case served as a precedent when the *New York Times* and *Washington Post* published the so-called Pentagon Papers. These important documents revealed information about the Vietnam War that the government hoped to keep secret. President Richard M. Nixon won a temporary court order barring publication of the Pentagon Papers. However, the newspapers appealed to the Supreme Court, which ruled that the government could not deny the press their right to publish the Pentagon Papers.

The ban against censorship in the form of prior restraint that came out of the *Saturday Press* case had now been applied in a case brought by two legitimate and widely read news sources. The Pentagon Papers decision is regarded as a key milestone in U.S. history of freedom of the press. Far less known, however, is that the Supreme Court's decision had its roots in a case involving an extremist press.

Virgil Griffin, imperial wizard of the Cleveland Knights of the Ku Klux Klan, is accompanied by security. Membership in the Klan is growing as illegal immigration increases.

TIMELINE

1798	1866	1901
John Fries organizes a rebellion of several hundred farmers to oppose a tax passed by Congress.	Six former Confederate soldiers found the Ku Klux Klan.	Anarchist Leon Czolgosz assassinates President William F. McKinley.

1934	1959	1969
Victor Houteff establishes a splinter group of the Seventh-day Adventist Church near Waco, Texas.	George Lincoln Rockwell founds the group that becomes the American Nazi Party.	The Supreme Court rules that only speech advocating a particular criminal act can be suppressed.

1917	1919	1931
Congress passes the Espionage Act, making it a crime to criticize U.S. involvement in World War I.	The Palmer Raids begin. Approximately 10,000 anarchists are deported.	The U.S. Supreme Court rules the government cannot exercise prior restraint over a publication.

1976	1978	1984
British animal rights activist Ronnie Lee founds the Animal Liberation Front.	White supremacist William Pierce publishes *The Turner Diaries*.	*Race and Reason*, produced by Ku Klux Klan leader Tom Metzger, debuts on cable television.

TIMELINE

1991

Operation Rescue harasses abortion clinic workers and clients for 46 days in Wichita, Kansas.

1993

On February 26, a jihadist group detonates a bomb in the parking garage of the World Trade Center in New York City.

1993

On April 19, the 51-day siege of the Branch Davidian complex ends.

2001

President Bush signs the USA Patriot Act on October 26.

2002

José Padilla is arrested on suspicion that he planned to detonate a dirty bomb in the United States.

1995	1999	2001
Timothy McVeigh and Terry Nichols explode a bomb in Oklahoma City, Oklahoma, killing 168 people.	Benjamin Nathaniel Smith goes on a murderous shooting spree in July.	On September 11, Islamic terrorists attack the United States and kill more than 3,000 people.

2007		2008
Federal authorities arrest six Islamic extremists for plotting an assault on Fort Dix in New Jersey.	.	John Taylor Bowles runs for president as the candidate of the extremist National Socialist Order of America.

Essential Facts

At Issue

Although extremist groups often promote agendas of racism, hate, and violence, members of extremist groups should enjoy the rights to free speech and assembly, as well as freedom of the press, as guaranteed to all U.S. citizens under the First Amendment. Dissident groups labeled as "extreme" create an interesting debate in a free democratic state. While laws protect such freedoms, they do not allow for violent actions or intimidations based on those same extreme beliefs.

A series of legislative and court rulings based on interpretations of the Constitution have ranged from making war criticisms illegal to upholding neo-Nazis' right to march. Extremist groups might pose potential security threats based on their beliefs, but until they take violent action and break the law, they remain protected by the law.

Critical Dates

1917
After Congress passed the Espionage Act, it became a crime to criticize or obstruct the war efforts. Many people in groups such as the Socialist Party considered this a violation of their civil rights. These objectors were labeled as threats to national security.

March 3, 1919
The Supreme Court ruled that the government may suppress speech only when it presents a clear and present danger.

January 22, 1973
The Supreme Court issued the *Roe v. Wade* decision that legalized abortion in the United States. This decision elicited violent actions by some extreme antiabortion groups.

June 14, 1978
Neo-Nazis won a court order permitting them to march in the predominantly Jewish suburb of Skokie, Illinois.

October 2001

Congress passed the USA Patriot Act. Some civil libertarians have called the act an infringement of civil rights.

QUOTES

In Favor

"I think we should be eternally vigilant against attempts to check the expression of opinions that we loathe and believe to be fraught with death, unless they so imminently threaten immediate interference with the lawful and pressing purposes of the law that an immediate check is required to save the country."—*U.S. Supreme Court Justice Oliver Wendell Holmes*

Opposed

"When he waded into that crowd on Saturday afternoon and tried to calm things down, he did not get a warm reception. A lot of people said, 'Man, you're black. You're one of us. Why did you let those neo-Nazis in here?'"—*Newspaper columnist Roberta de Boer, on the public's reaction to Toledo Mayor Jack Ford's decision to permit a neo-Nazi march*

ADDITIONAL RESOURCES

SELECT BIBLIOGRAPHY

Chowder, Ken, and Jeff Berlin. "The ACLU Defends Everybody." *Smithsonian*, Jan. 1998.

Cloud, John, and Julie Grace and Timothy Roche. "Is Hate on the Rise?" *Time*, 19 July 1999.

Dedman, Bill. "Midwest Gunman Had Engaged in Racist Acts at 2 Universities," *New York Times*, 6 July 1999.

Finan, Christopher M. *From the Palmer Raids to the Patriot Act: A History of the Fight for Free Speech in America*. Boston, MA: Beacon Press, 2007.

Hall, Christina. "Nazi Rally Sparks Protest, Prayer." *Toledo Blade*, 11 Dec. 2006.

Wade, Wyn Craig. *The Fiery Cross: The Ku Klux Klan in America*. Oxford, England: Oxford University Press, 1987.

Walker, Samuel. *In Defense of American Liberties: A History of the ACLU*. Oxford, England: Oxford University Press, 1990.

FURTHER READING

Isler, Claudia. *The Right to Free Speech*. New York, NY: Rosen Publishing Group, 2001.

Kjelle, Marylou Morano. *The Waco Siege*. Philadelphia, PA: Chelsea House Publishers, 2002.

Roleff, Tamara L., Ed. *Hate Groups: Opposing Viewpoints*. San Diego, CA: Greenhaven Press, 1999.

Sonder, Ben. *The Militia Movement: Fighters of the Far Right*. New York, NY: Franklin Watts, 2000.

Web Links

To learn more about extremist groups, visit ABDO Publishing
Company on the World Wide Web at **www.abdopublishing.com**.
Web sites about extremist groups are featured on our Book Links
page. These links are routinely monitored and updated to provide
the most current information available.

For More Information

For more information on this subject, contact or visit the following
organizations.

National Civil Rights Museum
450 Mulberry Street, Memphis, TN 38103
901-521-9699
www.civilrightsmuseum.org
This museum is located on the site where Martin Luther King Jr.
was assassinated in 1968. It includes exhibits about the struggle of
African Americans to win equal rights and resources on extremists.

National Constitution Center
Independence Mall, 525 Arch Street, Philadelphia, PA 19106
215-409-6600
www.constitutioncenter.org
This center is dedicated to the history of the Constitution and its
application to U.S. society. It features interactive exhibits that help
explain the Constitution's provisions, including the free speech
rights guaranteed under the First Amendment.

United States Holocaust Memorial Museum
100 Raoul Wallenberg Place Southwest, Washington DC
20024-2126
202-488-0400
www.ushmm.org
Learn about the ideology that drove the Nazi movement in World
War II-era Germany and has inspired neo-Nazi extremists in the
United States.

Glossary

anarchist
> One who believes government authority is unnecessary.

Aryan
> Currently, it is applied by Nazis to white, non-Jewish people of European descent.

Black Panther Party
> An African-American organization formed to promote self-reliance and civil liberties among African Americans, even if it results in violence.

civil liberties
> Freedoms that protect individuals from government actions. In the United States, these are stated in the Bill of Rights.

communists
> Political activists who seek a society based on collective ownership of property and the elimination of social classes.

ecoterrorist
> Someone who uses violence to further political changes for environmentalism.

electronic surveillance
> Use of wiretaps and other electronic devices, such as cameras and listening equipment, to secretly observe a criminal suspect.

espionage
> Spying or other secret efforts to undermine a government.

fascism
> A form of government in which individuals are subservient to the interests of the nation. A form of national unity based on ethnic, cultural, racial, or religious attributes.

House Un-American Activities Committee
> Investigative committee established by the U.S. House of Representatives in 1938 and disbanded in 1975. It was charged with exposing communist influence in U.S. society.

jihad
> Arabic word that means holy struggle.

Ku Klux Klan
An organization advocating white supremacy.

martial law
Law administered by force in an emergency to maintain public order and safety.

militia
Originally defined as a body of volunteer soldiers who served when called. More recently, secretive extremist groups that oppose government authority over the lives of citizens.

neo-Nazis
Individuals who have embraced Hitler's ideology following the defeat of the Nazi Germany regime in World War II.

Qur'an
The sacred scriptures of the Islamic religion, believed to contain revelations made to the Prophet Muhammad by God.

rhetoric
Communication through writing or speech.

socialists
Political activists who believe in the government ownership of the means of production and the distribution of goods.

vandalism
Criminal destruction of property, often committed by extremists to make political points.

vivisection
Medical research that employs surgery or other forms of experimentation on living animals.

warrant
Court order that permits an arrest, seizure of property, or surveillance on a suspect.

SOURCE NOTES

Chapter 1. The Right to Be Heard

1. Neal Conan. "Interview: Roberta de Boer Discusses Rioting in Toledo," *Talk of the Nation*, National Public Radio, 17 Oct. 2005.
2. Ibid.
3. Steve Mount. "United States Constitution." *The U.S. Constitution Online.* 23 Jan. 2008 <http://www.usconstitution.net/xconst_Am1. html>.
4. Christina Hall. "Nazi Rally Sparks Protest, Prayer." *Toledo Blade* 11 Dec. 2005. n. pag.

Chapter 2. Extremism in U.S. Society

1. Wyn Craig Wade. *The Fiery Cross: The Ku Klux Klan in America.* Oxford, England: Oxford University Press, 1987. 126.
2. Christopher M. Finan. *From the Palmer Raids to the Patriot Act: A History of the Fight for Free Speech in America.* Boston: Beacon Press, 2007. 33.

3. Ibid.

Chapter 3. Defending the Rights of Extremists

1. "Quotation #331." The Quotations page. 28 Jan. 2008 <http:// www.quotationspage.com/quote/331.html>.
2. "Freedom of Expression—ACLU Position Paper" 2 Jan. 1997. 8 Apr. 2008 <http://www.aclu.org/freespeech/>.
3. Samuel Walker. *In Defense of American Liberties: A History of the ACLU.* Oxford, England: Oxford University Press, 1990. 80.
4. Ibid. 323.

Chapter 4. Crossing the Rhetorical Line

1. "The Great Creator," *Southern Poverty Law Center Intelligence Report,* Summer 1999, <http://www.splcenter.org/intel/intelreport/article. jsp?pid=569>.
2. John Cloud, Julie Grace, and Timothy Roche. "Is Hate on the Rise?" *Time* 19 July 1999. 33.
3. "Pontifex, Esq.," *Southern Poverty Law Center Intelligence Report* Spring 1999, <http://www.splcenter.org/intel/intelreport/article. jsp?aid=354>.
4. Bill Dedman. "Midwest Gunman Had Engaged in Racist Acts at 2 Universities." *New York Times* 6 July 1999. A-1.
5. "Pontifex, Esq.," *Southern Poverty Law Center Intelligence Report,*

Spring 1999, <http://www.splcenter.org/intel/intelreport/article. jsp?aid=354>.

6. "The Hate Crimes Question." PBS NewsHour, 11 Aug. 1999. 6 Feb. 2008 <http://www.pbs.org/newshour/bb/law/july-dec99/ hate_8-11.html>.

7. "Matthew Hale Gets Maximum 40-Year Sentence." *Southern Poverty Law Center Intelligence Report,* Spring 1999. <http://www.splcenter.org/intel/news/ item.jsp?site_area=1&aid=102>.

Chapter 5. Is Force Justified?

1. Stuart A. Wright, Ed. *Armageddon in Waco: Critical Perspectives on the Branch Davidian Conflict.* Chicago: University of Chicago Press, 1995. 319.

2. Lou Michael and Dan Herbeck. *American Terrorist: Timothy McVeigh and the Oklahoma City Bombing.* New York: ReganBooks, 2001.121.

Chapter 6. Spreading the Extremist Message

1. Christopher M. Finan. *From the Palmer Raids to the Patriot Act: A History of the Fight for Free Speech in America.* Boston: Beacon Press, 2007. 29.

2. "The Gun Network: Excerpts from One Right-Wing Author's Script for the Future." *New York Times* 5 July 1995. A-18.

3. "William Pierce." *Times of London* 16 Aug. 2002. n. pag.

4. "Klan Wins a Battle for Cable TV." *New York Times* 16 July 1989. A-20.

5. Russell Working. "Illegal Abroad, Hate Web Sites Thrive Here." *Chicago Tribune* 13 Nov. 2007. n. pag.

6. John Sutherland. "Gospels of Hate that Slip Through the Net." *The Guardian* 3 Apr. 2000. 6 Feb.2008 <http://www.guardian.co/ uk/mcveigh/story/0,7369,488284,00.html>.

Chapter 7. Abortion Opposition

1. Randall Terry. *Operation Rescue.* Pittsburgh, PA: Whitaker House, 1988. Reprinted in Bruno Leone, Ed., *The Abortion Controversy.* San Diego, CA: Greenhaven Press, 1995. 184.

2. Kimberly Sevcik. "One Man's God Squad." *Rolling Stone* 19 Aug. 2004. 108.

3. Dallas A. Blanchard and Terry J. Prewitt. *Religious Violence and*

Source Notes Continued

Abortion: The Gideon Project. Gainesville, FL: University Press of Florida, 1993. 259.

4. Joseph Scheidler. *Closed: 99 Ways to Stop Abortion.* Rockford, IL: Tan Publishers, 1993. Reprinted in Leone, Ed., *The Abortion Controversy.* 191.

Chapter 8. Protecting the Planet

1. Patrick Range McDonald. "Monkey Madness at UCLA." *LA Weekly* 8 Aug. 2007, <http://www.laweekly.com/news/news/monkey-madness-at-ucla/16986>.

2. Debra J. Saunders. "American Terrorist." *San Francisco Chronicle* 5 July 2007. n. pag.

3. "Ecoterrorism: Extremism in the Animal Rights and Environmentalist Movements," Anti-Defamation League Law Enforcement Agency Resource Network. 14 Mar. 2008 <http://www.adl.org/Learn/Ext_US/Ecoterrorism.asp>.

4. Ibid.

5. Brad Knickerbocker. "'Ecoterrorism' Stirs Debate." *Christian Science Monitor* 18 May 2007. 2-2.

Chapter 9. Jihadists in the United States

1. Jerry Markon. "Virginia Jihad Case Hailed as Key in War on Terror," *Washington Post* 8 June 2006. A-3.

2. Hassan Isilow. "Islam Denounces Terror." *Kampala Monitor* 22 Apr. 2007 <http://allafrica.com/stories/200704230301.html>.

3. Harun Yahya. "The Pacifism of Islam." 23 May 2004. < http://www.readingislam.com/servlet/Satellite?c=Article_C&cid=1154235111200&pagename=Zone-English-Discover_Islam%2FDIELayout>.

4. Jerry Markon. "Virginia Jihad Case Hailed as Key in War on Terror." *Washington Post* 8 June 2006. A-3.

5. Jenny Cuffe. "U.S. Muslims 'Alienated by Patriot Act.'" BBC News, 4 July 2004, <http://news.bbc.co.uk/2/hi/programmes/file_on_4/5145970.stm>.

6. George Anastasia. "6 Held in Terror Plot." *Philadelphia Inquirer,* 9 May 2007. A-1.

7. Todd Steven Burroughs. "The ACLU on Preserving Civil Liberties." *New Crisis* Nov.-Dec. 2001. 13.

8. Associated Press. "Store Clerk Helps Feds Bust 6 in Alleged 'Jihad' Plot to Kill U.S. Soldiers at Fort Dix." 8 May 2007. <http://www.foxnews.com/story/0,2933,270601,00.html>
9. Bill Cunningham. "In the Spirit: Theology and Terrorism Cloud Islam's Reach." *Orange County Register* 11 Jan. 2008, < http://www.ocregister.com/life/alqaida-qazwini-terrorism-1958014-muslims-islam>.
10. Jerry Markon. "Virginia Jihad Case Hailed as Key in War on Terror." *Washington Post* 8 June 2006. A-3.
11. "ACLU Says President Bush Misled Public on Patriot Act; Urges Congress to Bring Law in Line with the Constitution," American Civil Liberties Union news release, 9 June 2005 <http://www.aclu.org/safefree/general/17650prs20050609.html>.

Chapter 10. New Sparks to Extremism

1. "Ku Klux Klan Rebounds with New Focus on Immigration, ADL Reports." Anti-Defamation League news release, 6 Feb. 2007. <http://www.adl.org/PresRele/Extremism_72/4973_72.htm>.
2. Corey Hutchins. "S.C. Nazi for President?" *Columbia City Paper*, 14 Feb. 2007. <http://www.columbiacitypaper.com/2007/2/15/s-c-nazi-for-president>.
3. Lee Higgins. "Neo-Nazi Group to Rally at Capitol," *The State*, 15 Apr. 2007. n. pag.
4. Ku Klux Klan Rebounds with New Focus on Immigration, ADL Reports," Anti-Defamation League news release, 6 Feb. 2007. <http://www.adl.org/PresRele/Extremism_72/4973_72.htm>.

INDEX

ABOUT THE AUTHOR

Hal Marcovitz is a former newspaper reporter who has written more than 100 books for young readers. In 2005, *Nancy Pelosi*, his biography of House Speaker Nancy Pelosi, was named to *Booklist* magazine's list of recommended feminist books for young readers. He has won three Keystone Press Awards, the highest award for newspaper reporting presented by the Pennsylvania Newspaper Association. He lives in Pennsylvania with his family.

PHOTO CREDITS

Carolyn Kaster/AP Images, cover; Daniel Miller/AP Images, 6; Kiichiro Sato/AP Images, 9; Bill Pugliano/Stringer/Getty Images, 15; AP Images, 16, 21, 27; Bettmann/Corbis, 28; AP Images, 33; William Campbell/Sygma/Corbis, 35; Fred Zwicky/AP Images, 36; Kari Shuda/AP Images, 43; Ron Heflin/AP Images, 44; David J. Phillip/AP Images, 51; David Longstreath/AP Images, 52; David S. Holloway/Getty Images, 59; Joe Marquett/AP Images, 60; Mark Lennihan/AP Images, 67; Peter Lennihan/AP Images, 68; Elizabeth Armstrong/AP Images, 75; Matthew Cavanaugh/AP Images, 76; Andrew Shepard/AP Images, 83; Charles Dharapak/AP Images, 87; Al Henkel/AP Images, 88; Rick Glickstein/AP Images, 95